A Caterpillar on the Leaf

A Caterpillar On The Leaf
L Ghazals

Rae Desmond Jones

PUNCHER & WATTMANN

First published in 2016

Published by Puncher & Wattmann
PO Box 441
Glebe NSW 2037

http://www.puncherandwattmann.com
puncherandwattmann@bigpond.com

National Library of Australia
Cataloguing in Publication entry:

Jones, Rae Desmond

A Caterpillar on the Leaf

ISBN   9781922186645

I. Title

A821.3

Cover design by Matthew Holt

Printed by Lightning Source International

This project has been assisted by the Australian Government through the Australia Council, its arts funding and advisory body.

Australian Government

Australia Council
for the Arts

i.m. Dr. Patricia Brennan

I

to the beloved on the last night

in the dark a woman knits across the table,
       her needles click softly & tenderly.

the smell of roses are rich & sweet,
       the pulsing blood of moving air.

the old pepper tree shudders & whispers,
       the full moon spills silver into my hands.

shadow, what do you know?
       the sinistral mirror smiles along its crack.

the sparkling stars peck at the clouds,
       an angel breathes down my back.

there is no one else in all there is
       & our world is alone in its wick of light.

II

in my memory twin girls stand side by side
   with open wide light blue eyes.

if they were one i could have loved her
   with her four eyed spaniel gaze.

but i was one although there was another
   moving secretly behind my two eyes.

a fawning image moved there slow & willing
   to strangle my twin & to kill.

those double girls still stand before me,
   staring through me to my twin.

III

death was such good fun-
  booze, drugs & poetry.

how did i avoid you?
  so Byronic, so good looking!

i've grown old & lucky
  but still there's too many of me,

scratching marks on paper, computers,
  Beethoven, the horses of Lascaux.

there's wars for the young but
  still our population grows.

spring, & purple flowers spatter the horizon -
  i like it here & don't want to leave

IV

leaves mulch my concrete pathway:
        somewhere in the roof there is a rat.

after this year's winter storms
        the gutters & downpipes block & overflow.

a rough pyramid of sandstone could make a wall
        if i would dig a deep neat trench.

citrus trees produce sweet fruit,
        small oranges, fat grapefruit, oozing lemons.

as we sleep Eden grows around us,
        weeds & bright coloured singing birds.

V

your hairdryer cracks the morning sky
        into veins of diamond light.

along this valley of slowing hearts
        polished mirrors whisper reply.

i remember, therefore i am,
        recalling you as you are.

a timid God hides meekly
        behind a G-string of cloud.

the black taxi waits as the radio sings
        there may be no tomorrow.

VI

alone with her mirror,
    too much pancake & lipstick.

in the empty hairdresser's shop a girl
    watches me pass.

an image glowers back to front, left to right
    insolent eyes, unruly hair.

her eyes are dark & should be beautiful:
    what causes her to hate me?

she is no body to me as i walk on,
    hand in hand with the dead.

VII

without your imagined prescience
    the unlocked gate claps in the wind.

in a universe emptied of meaning
    Suns collide against the iron walls of time.

how the storm beats the roof,
    cars creep by − wombats in the mist.

each month i have lost a friend,
    this is the time of winnowing.

above the clouds i conjure my harvest -
    the light, the darkness & the stars.

VIII

a fair woman behind her fan
        interrogates our string quartet as they start to tune.

the Sahara draws a bow slowly across strings of air,
        a thick drone of abundance.

guests arrive yet they do not eat
        although we have laid a princely table.

bubbles exhale from dry sparkling wine,
        her honey light hair.

why are there no lovers?
        who is that stranger sawing tent ropes?

a peacock screams from our garden edge:
        two lions watch from the road.

IX

each spring a transparent double
       watches closely & she smiles.

in washed out light a frightened cloud
       skirts the trembling borders of heaven.

deep manured shadows whisper
       from sweet tended flowerbeds.

my skin is patched & frayed,
       i step carefully into my disrobed past -

ancient trees nod as i pass,
       their knotted arms rise in prayer.

recall that splintered broken door,
       did she curse me as she died?

X

a line of ash blondes puff out their cheeks
       & seven trumpets wail.

so the boy with a ponytail
       allows a cheeky oboe to kiss his lips.

five double basses pluck delicately
       to add a sombre touch.

the conductor leans forward,
       his fingers stroke the border of silence.

Scheherazade dances as she sings,
       the Sultan's body rises to the ceiling.

perfect lines of silence intersect
       at an intangible empty place.

spores of life drift there
       on the winds of gravity.

an unmanned microscope
       pans the abundant heavens.

living storms of dust
       seek a cool desolate moon.

free at last from speech, grave syllables
       drink & dance & fornicate.

XI

Bessie Smith sings Oh Careless Love
        on the radio – i stop the car.

the music forms a shell about me,
        she sang this 15 years before I was born.

i heard it before, but i did not.
        that voice a raw symphony:

like Beethoven, her power swells,
        the cabin pulses to the beat of blood.

i am stunned by desire:
        the joy, the hunger of it.

XII

there are Suns out there, far away,
        blinking their personal code of grief.

they whisper fire, then darkness, searching,
        but the speed of light is slow.

they weep in shock of that cremation
        separating them from their Mother,

she who clenched her children in her centre
        until the great auto-da-fe of gravity.

beloved creatrix & destroyer,
        all things will return to you:

in the background your afterglow -
        the light & dust of our creation.

XIII

rainbow of oil on a wet black road:
        i know you are watching me.

you are protected by satellite,
        camera surveillance & stainless steel.

desire survives when i am gone
        in the form of a small grey cloud.

over the iron fence a pomegranate hangs:
        i take it, shake it, pull it free.

i adore this world:
        my wine & my downfall.

XIV

in the heat of the day she comes when i hide beneath a sheet,
   she is so small yet her bite breaks my skin.

she feeds & draws blood from the deep well of my existence.
   why hide from a fly in a shroud of whiteness?

i want to escape your bite, God, yet you will never let me go!
   like God you are everywhere, small yet limitless.

yes, i believe in your emptiness, the depth of your frail existence:
   you are nothing – i imagine you not here, but you are back:

i can not kill you, fly God, nor can i live with you.
   i experience your fullness & mysterious emptiness.

you hum your mantra in my ear,
   the itch of space & light & time.

XV

i drive a dream Ferrari
        with a loose steering wheel.

my Father waves from the front row
        beside his ancestors.

sunlight touches a scratch of glass,
        a scream of light.

i don't seem to be going fast
        but neutral stars burn & disappear.

my mob cheers as i take the curve -
        this is my body.

XVI

my pen drips dark blue ink,
        hungry rivers break their banks.

deep clefts of my making
        are as distant as the Moon,

words which slide & fail
        the depth of my adoration.

i fear your interrogation
        now everything is lost to you.

along the broad leaf of the vine a caterpillar
        eats his way to the heart.

XVII

boys on skateboards scour concrete paths,
        balanced carelessly in their centripetal youth.

young women in short skirts sway on spider legs,
        pale with winter.

old men sit around our village square to get drunk
        & throw bottles joyfully at the wall.

a grey Greek in his cap plays old music on a saxophone
        – it fills the street with honey.

the pervading smell of jasmine from each strangled fence
        prophecies Summer's sweet corruption.

XVIII

to a riff of stand by your man a bright red can
        rolls down the glaring concrete.

council guy in a yellow fluoro jacket
        chops the air as he talks in Arabic to his empty hand.

a woman in thongs wheels a wobbly pram,
        "you want my wife?" her man snarls in my face.

dripping with sweat & coca cola,
        our failing bodies are not enough.

beyond the road, love's old sweet song as sparrows
        feed on the sweat of an ancient tree.

the name of God is inadequate
        unless we understand her manifest wit.

two dozen butts rise in the breeze in perfect time
        as automatic doors slide open.

XIX

he opens an album of the farm.
       his life is sepia & it glows.

sand builds & smears the lens,
       he feels it hard along his veins.

where are those Clydesdales now?
       they took them to that war.

he is there, not here
       because there is warm & sun.

singing nurse swings open the door,
       a steel bedpan draped in a towel.

XX

think iron circles touching
       in the dry chemistry of space.

impossible to believe —
       i watch the rise of a smouldering Sun.

time breathes out & bulging galaxies
       pop their eyeballs.

a dry leaf shudders in the wind
       afraid it can't live forever.

would you need an extra day
       to gain wisdom & strength?

XXI

the moving finger taps then hits save,
        i send it on email.

europe slips into crisis
        not for the first or last time.

is this the rise of Asia,
        the fall of Western Rome?

my father went down the mines in 1931 —
        he might have been an accountant.

a hungry future
        whispers through my dreams.

outside in the dark rain old eucalypts bend
        then spring back,

droplets spit at my window
        & dribble to feed the fertile dirt.

there are many refugees lost in this storm —
        they are human, as are we.

XXII

we are chosen & by what right
        dare you remain silent?

the streets are quiet
        except for the sweepers,

those untouchables who speak
        with the whisper of brooms.

announcements are distributed
        on yellow paper from corners.

we are unused to speech since
        your tongue stopped our mouths.

through broken sewers under sunken roads
        our waste returns,

we have created you in our image:
        all of this belongs to us.

XXIII

dream dim familiar lanes
      & paths bright with broken glass.

a cracking concrete dam, a bar of lead
      between your shoulder blades.

lie quiet in the dark, wait
      for the globe to flicker off.

below the mosquito's syncopation
      wait & watch, watch & wait.

it seemed so long – you forget -
      were you really there?

XXIV

air force 1 hits the tarmac
        as huns bang politely against the gates.

turn the lock, open the sluice -
        why fight when they could buy us out?

confucius' wisdom is as great as the bible
        & there are fewer Thou shalt nots.

the Emperor's speech inspires us all
        to sign the paper − forget the mines.

our Roman armies may march North through deserts
        where riches bleed beneath the earth.

bulldozers scrape empty the guts of time,
        they dig our fortune & our grave.

XXV

above our car park the clouds
      rub in wanton spring frottage.

a steaming downpour –
      all the juice of heaven.

beads of frost swell & pearl
      before they roll & unite,

listlessly dripping down to earth –
      then pool & sulk.

see them stare back at the storm,
      aching to embrace the Sun.

XXVI

onions steeped in brown vinegar,
        voluptuous bottoms pressed against glass.

tomatoes express that colour
        from embarrassment at our behaviour.

pineapples jump up to the ceiling
        to enliven a flaccid un-sprung Sun.

figs hang in rows with stems dripping cream -
        brown scrotums of aging men.

dried apricots' erotic gleam,
        vulvas slippery with their lust.

potatoes sit shrouded by the dirt we came from
        to remind us to be humble.

beans that are soaked in tins
        drop drowned & sobbing on our plate.

think gently of your fruits & veges,
        they might be your grandparent's souls.

XXVII

do you watch houris shimmy through
        rose coloured glasses as you rise to the ceiling?

how long can a spark in your drying brain
        fire those vixens in the freezing film of space time?

already those compliant virgins laugh goodbye -
        their hymens grow back each time.

the hungry jealousy you hide turns in you –
        you think you can destroy the world.

someone important waits outside the bordello
        as grieving relatives walk to their cars.

XXVIII

on the seat outside our grand exeloo
        a line of grey men wait & talk.

out of the supermarket's open mouth
        a woman wheels a trolley of toilet paper.

a blonde in pink panties glides on a skateboard,
        trailing clouds of hash as she goes.

old men remember the tree which stood,
        a good shop that burned.

consider motivation, insurance & economics,
        cost of petrol & cigarettes.

two fat pigeons enthroned on the fountain
        splash with joyous disdain.

XXIX

that chalky lady leaning on the table
       touches her lips.

she never needed paint —
       now death smudges those violet eyes.

then, she did not walk — men stared.
       she floated in their eyes.

i lean & touch her wrist -
       her laugh is light & young.

in a painting on the wall,
       white winter flowers.

XXX

Italia / Campione Del Mondo 2006,
      all of that indestructible juicy potency.

bolder even than all the sultry young men
      with airbrushed hair around the wall.

a line of ancient warriors on their seats
      look mildly into the marbled mirror -

watch closely shelves of oil, pomades,
      scissors & a fluted silver black blow drier.

there rests the razor, there stands
      a grizzled shaving brush, with fretted hairs.

our barber severs a mop of dark lustrous hair
      & it descends in clumps to the grey slate floor.

XXXI

the hard top rolls back: you pose modestly, hand raised,
        sunlight glinting on the white teeth of your smile.

your silver Bentley rolls along Governor Macquarie's road ,
        nudging Fords & Hondas, General Motors & Hyundai,

though they honk & bellow as they always have,
        you know, frog-mouthed Caesar, you must die,

yet always in the heart of temporal power is no,
        a subterranean whisper – distinct beneath that applause,

cheers echoing as the shallow air breathes -
        a taut rope, strapping down the equator of our world.

XXXII

a vee of sparrows cross a deep night sky,
        the full moon cracks in half, a broken biscuit.

is that thick cloud rolling in from the West —
        or my cervical vertebrae sliding beneath?

does the ceiling move inexorably down or
        is that double bed rising, swift as an elevator?

with a computer guided missile, you don't need
        a compass to find the city,or a man to aim?

from the next ward down, old men talk -
        their dreams & nightmares will soon pass

XXXIII

you have been waiting
        quiet as ever, my friend.

although i have never seen your face
        you are near me.

so close, the warm breath
        of your need.

i too have been waiting,
        although i did not know you.

i glimpsed you once
        with the light behind you.

my body is afraid as i go
        to meet an unknown lover.

XXXIV

that thing that is not me
           has intelligence, will & yearning.

he wants to live & love
           & whisper jokes to me at night.

why so cruel & hungry?
           he is my cruelty & hunger.

he pretends to be my friend
           but i am his food.

when the doctors open me
           they will meet my sweet baby.

tonight the moon is red –
           rest in the cradle of my flesh.

XXXV

the lights of town fall behind me
        as foothills rise.

a smell of eucalypt on the breeze,
        last year's leaves crack underfoot.

within their camoulflage of trees
        a thousand lizards click.

your remembered words become clear
        in this dry alpine air.

imagine silence breaking
        through an orchestra of birds.

there is a broken hut up here
        where i can build a fire.

XXXVI

the Wolf paws her photos
    with his desire & need to know -

a badge of a singing bird on her heart,
    ring finger forward —

behind her a keyboard & a glowing lamp
    — an iridescent expanding universe,

a fragile sweet smile
    on that sensitive laughing face.

such elegance, so steeped in life,
    she conjures a dance of invisible delight.

XXXVII

you should not appear within my dreams
        except to declare portents or turn up the cards,

nor (as beautiful as you are) remain insensible
        to conventions applying in my lethargic dreams,

retaining all garments & decency intact.
        my dreams are reserved for scenes of seduction

& the occasional Bachanal where frenzied
        bourgeois bay at the gates of the Senate.

why venture where i speak with the dead,
        those who whisper love & stand with open hands,

reminding me of some duty that i forgot -
        an anniversary of a blame, a love, or death?

XXXVIII

our parents have gone,
          probing flashlights into the grave.

those forbidden corners of desire
          flash boldly on daytime television.

when two young lovers die for lust -
          it's Romeo & Juliet on page five.

death of a starlet or the drug addled young
          might make it to page three.

Jonathan Swift suggested eating babies
          to solve the Irish problem.

XXXIX

on flaming tyres an outlaw cruises
   to her chosen Calvary.

sad facsimiles of antique citizens
   nod through transparent glass,

primeval yellow masks daubed
   in pious regret.

along our freeways snoring motorbikes go silent
   as that lovely outlaw passes.

a nagging wind corrodes that small bare hill
   where beats the heart.

XL

pale city lights behind him,
        pink lipstick on that cloud.

tall & thin those canvas shoes
        make no sound,

he stands still before my headlights
        & stares back into me.

i could drive over him
        (would it be murder?)

our street rolls out behind him,
        a long tongue of forever.

he hasn't shaved for a week:
        what questions does he ask?

the whites of his eyes,
        no moon, the darkness.

XLI

An afternoon storm drenches our clothes line,
      my shirt flaps mute & white.

each leaf on the orange tree flutters
      as it drips, drips, drips.

a spider weaves between the trees,
      each web snatches a shaft of light.

silver coins in dark air,
      lines of uncut grass tremble.

a passenger jet hovers like a shark
      as lightning twinkles along his steel body.

XLII

half asleep with the window open
        a Southerly wind quakes the house

gusts of rain spit on my manuscript
        storm of pages swirl about the floor

today the sky sparkled as
        clouds chased each other.

i write outraged at the freezing bare arse of it
        all the way from Antarctica

when all i asked for was a polite opinion
        on climate change

XLIII

squabbling birds around a low shrub:
         poets feed on a single blossom

whose mobile telephone chimes Mozart
         through a grey cement wall?

millions of our young have died
         of brave delusion –

they, who will never face television,
         plain age & wisdom.

grapefruit falls from the tree,
         skulls bleach in the Sun.

trucks carry cans of coca cola –
         counterfeit wine & blood

XLIV

what are the dreams of boys?
        a burning itch between the legs,

galleons loaded down with silver
        in a rising storm.

waves of dopamine — images
        of naked houris dancing.

pull down the temple, hold up the head,
        eternal consolation of the breast.

babies & nappies, sleepless nights.
        is reality what it was about?

old bugger dreams surge & storm,
        a hungry ocean.

absurd & cruel this selfish oaf
        dreams of writhing women,

a dismal hope squirts in the genes —
        lord or demon of my brain,

if you exist here or beyond the stars,
        make me indifferent, brave & wise.

XLV

my wardrobe door gapes & smiles,
   old timber gums.

you are lucky to be alive
   the air conditioner whines.

i am alone & dream of you,
   together we cannot dream.

careful people
   are those i love least.

when there are no surprises
   what is trust?

XLVI

so kinky & slinky
           is that sexy old Sun,

he warms the air
           & makes her dance

& whacks her bottom
           with a playful smack.

it is so sweet music
           i wish my voice

was deep & rippled
           so i could sing

up into the shivery sky
           deep baritone notes,

o fun of life, the sheer
           tragic bullshit of it.

XLVII

bald, with his shaven head
       he might be a nazi or a saint.

he is in there, wandering
       through my pituitary,

a ghost with loaded forms
       gliding & grinning -

a broken bottle – a razor,
       a head kicked soft as a pumpkin.

he shuffles toward me, draped
       in seepage from my brain.

a droplet of fear dribbles
       into an ocean of poison.

i am ready to break his flicking arm
       & roll him on the concrete path.

his grey boyish eyes look into me
       shocking in their nakedness.

XLVIII

no point discussing poetry,
        it is what it says.

stars kiss — dissolving planets
        breathe through darkness.

through the glass
        i love my pornographic self,

obscene images of creation,
        coupling, birthing, fire.

on the sweat of earth's rough skin
        oceans dance & brawl,

now a dying body snatches
        at the light.

XLIX

as my party goes on
        alluring music drones.

a lovely woman from years ago
        begins to nautch in the light.

she hasn't changed a bit despite
        decades of booze & babies.

I want to dance with her again
        but i am wedged into the chair

of memory, impotent inside my dream.
        i feed on you, imago, Shakti, desire.

L

my seed pushes beneath the earth
      unable to break the crust.

still i do what i want to want,
      dipping into the stunted bag of 'i can'.

an old eagle watches from the rock,
      thinking 'what is meaning? did i create it?'

always that girl with long red hair
      scrapes a drum with a furry stick.

there are lots of them have gone that way –
      i will follow them soon enough.

Acknowledgements

I would like to express my gratitude to joanne burns, Alyse Jones & Cecilia White for their generous comments on this manuscript.

Chazal 1 was published in *Decline And Fall* (ASM Press 2011) and several others in slightly different form in *Mascara* and *Melaleucca*. Ghazal XXI was published on *Poetry Breakfast* (US).

www.ingramcontent.com/pod-product-compliance
Lightning Source LLC
Chambersburg PA
CBHW031007090426
42737CB00008B/715